Kiwi
Adventures

Kiwi
Adventures

Bartha Hill

CF4·K

© Copyright 2007 Bartha Hill
ISBN 978-1-84550-282-9
Published in 2007
by
Christian Focus Publications,
Geanies House, Fearn, Tain,
Ross-shire, IV20 1TW,
Great Britain
Cover design by Daniel van Straaten
Cover illustration by Graham Kennedy
Other illustrations by Fred Apps

Scripture taken from the *New International Version* (NIV)
Copyright ©1988, 1989, 1991
by Tyndale House Publishers, Inc. Wheaton, IL 60189
Scripture taken from the *Contemporary English Version* (CEV)
Copyright © American Bible Society, 1995
by American Bible Society
Scripture taken from *The Message* (TM)
Copyright © 2007
by Navpress Publishing Company
Used by permission.

Printed in Wales by CPD

Contents

New Zealand

New Zealand is a long narrow country to the East of Australia between the Tasman Sea and the Pacific Ocean. It has three main islands: the North Island, the South Island and Stewart Island.

It is a land of high mountains, mighty flowing rivers and thermal springs. Between the West and East Coasts of the South Island is a range of snow-capped mountains known as the Southern Alps or The Great Divide. The tallest mountain is Aoraki or Mount Cook which is 3,754 metres high. Many people will agree that the most beautiful is Mount Aspiring.

The highest mountains in the north island are on the central volcanic plateau: Mount Ruapehu is 2,797 metres, Mount Tongariro is 1,978 metres and Mount Ngauruhoe is 2,291 metres. These mountains are active and erupt from time to time.

Further west is a beautiful cone shaped mountain called Mount. Taranaki. Although it is a dormant volcano scientists believe it will erupt one day soon and the people living in the town below it, New Plymouth, are used to its regular rumbling.

New Zealand's many ski fields are popular with overseas visitors, but there are also many other opportunities for adventure: hikes through the rugged mountain areas, jet boating, fly fishing, and more. There is a group of young trampers who carry two or three extra Bibles in their packs and leave them in remote mountain huts. Often the minds of lonely hikers spending days waiting for wild weather to calm turn to the God who created the magnificent world they see around them. 'When I consider your heavens, the work of your fingers, the moon and the stars, which you have set in place, what is man that you are mindful of him, the son of man that you care for him?' it says in Psalm 8:3,4.

Of course you don't have to go to the mountains to see some of the wonders of God's creation. Even in a busy city you can look up at the night sky to see the countless stars that God has placed there. Or you can visit the city gardens and touch some of the wonderful trees or look at the flowers. What other things help you think about God and His creation? And how can you say thank you to God for these wonderful gifts?

New Zealand is the only country in the world where you can find flightless birds like the Kiwi, Pukeko, Weka and Takahe, as well as other fascinating birds, penguins and lizards. Fortunately for campers, there are no snakes!

New Zealanders are often called Kiwis because nowhere in the world is there an animal quite like the Kiwi! Unlike the bird, human kiwis fly everywhere to live and work in almost every country in the world, but dream of coming home one day. New Zealand is well-known across the world for many things - great scenery, wildlife, travel, and even film sets. New Zealand is also famous for its national rugby team called the All Blacks. This team has a distinctive black uniform with a silver fern motif. The team is also well known for performing the traditional Maori dance called the Haka before all their matches.

The first people to come to New Zealand were the Maori who arrived around the thirteenth century in large canoes from other countries in the Pacific. When they saw the long strip of cloud from the distance they called it Aotearoa, the land of the long white cloud. They settled all over the three islands and brought with them sweet potatoes, and the ability to hunt and make fire. They hunted the giant moa and other birds and fished for food.

They also brought rats and dogs. The country's flightless birds were easy prey for these animals and fire destroyed many of their habitats. Within a short time thirty-two bird species disappeared forever. Another nine disappeared after the first European settlers arrived with ferrets and cats.

European settlers didn't arrive until the seventeenth century, when a dutch sea captain, Abel Tasman, sailed round the three islands of New Zealand. At that time cartographers and geographers believed that there was an unknown Southern Continent known by the name 'Terra Australis Incognita'. Tasman's instructions were to find it and come back with a list of new places to trade in gold, silver, spices and fabrics.

Somehow, while sailing east from Mauritius, Tasman didn't even find Australia, except for its southern and eastern tip now known as Tasmania. Eight days later he sighted New Zealand.

He landed at the northern part of the south island and in the north island where he was scared away by the Maori. He named the country 'Zelandia Nova' which later became New Zealand. But he did not find 'Terra Australis Incognita'.

It was not till 126 years later that an English sea captain, James Cook, sailed from Tahiti to rediscover the land discovered by Tasman. His job was also to look for 'Terra Australis Incognito'. The Royal Society of England told him that any native people he might come across on his journeys had been created by the same God as his own people. He was to treat them with great respect and not to take over any part of their country without their permission. James Cook took these directions seriously.

It took Cook six months to sail round the country on his ship 'Endeavour'. In all, he visited New Zealand four times and made accurate and careful maps, some of which are still in use today.

Among the crew on Cook's ship was a naturalist, Joseph Banks. Joseph loved to get up early in the morning and listen to the birds singing. Once, when the Endeavour lay at anchor in Queen Charlotte Sound he commented that the singing of the birds had awoken him. He had no idea how many of them there were, but they made the most melodious wild music he had ever heard, with sounds like small silver bells. But what he heard was a mere echo of what he might have heard 400 years earlier, for by 1770 around half of the native bird species were already extinct.

In the Garden of Eden, God gave Adam and Eve charge over His wonderful creation, but when they disobeyed and sin came in they had to leave the Garden. Ever since, the purity of nature has been damaged or destroyed by the sinful actions of man.

Because sin came into the world even our best efforts can not make our world as perfect as what God created. Even though we may not mean to, the effects of what we do can harm our bodies, families, environment, even the future. But there is hope. On a mountain called Calvary, Jesus changed everything. Although the wages of sin are death, because of Calvary God gives those who repent and believe in his Son eternal life. You can read about this in Romans 6:23.

But let's start our adventure on the east coast from where we will travel south along the rugged coast to Dunedin, through the wilderness area of the Catlins Coast, down to Invercargill, and across Foveaux Straight to Stewart Island. Then we will travel along the south coast and head north to Lakes Te Anau, Manapouri, Whakatipu and Wanaka.

Courage and Ingenuity

Because New Zealand is an island nation, at one time you could only reach it by boat, but today Timaru has an airport. It has an interesting connection with the beginnings of flight.

Just outside Timaru is the small town of Waitohi where one of the world's first six aviators was born in 1877. Many believe Richard Pearse flew his plane on 1 April 1903, a few months before the Wright Brothers succeeded at Kitty Hawk (17 December 1903). Richard was only twenty-five years old at the time.

Even as a very small boy Richard was different to his six brothers and sisters. He loved to tinker with everything mechanical. He read every book and magazine he could find on engineering and chemistry even when he was walking behind a plough!

He liked to make special presents for his family: he made a mechanical needle threader for his mother, his sisters were fascinated by a zoetrope that produced moving images by flicking through a series of still pictures, and for his brothers he made a small steam engine from a golden syrup tin filled with water. Using a small methylated spirits burner made from a small glass bottle with a cloth wick to heat the water, steam pushed on a little piston rotated a flywheel which made the engine spin very fast, emitting small puffs of steam.

One day he surprised his friends at school with a primitive helicopter, consisting of a baseboard with a nail on it, a cotton reel, a piece of string and the top of a herring tin cut and twisted into a propeller. When he wound the string around the reel and tugged on it the tin propeller shot off from the nail. When he was fifteen years old he patented his design for a bicycle, made of bamboo with pedals that moved up and down only. Six years later he built a four-speed motorcycle.

His ingenuity knew no bounds. He used whatever scraps he could find to make his inventions. This was not unusual because New Zealanders are well known for using scraps of all sorts to make things they need. It is known as 'Kiwi Ingenuity'. But with Richard it was more than that. He was fascinated by the idea of flying. He began to make planes when he was just twelve years old. He persuaded the town blacksmith to forge a crankshaft and turn the pistons for a small engine he made on a home-made lathe, using irrigation pipe for the two cylinders. Then he built a two cylinder horizontally opposed air cooled engine of about fifteen horse power.

Richard used bamboo, linen and other scraps to make his first plane with a puller propeller made from the metal of sheep dip drums. He didn't manage to fly it but that didn't stop him trying! He continued to improve the models and finally, in 1903, he flew one at a height of about 4 metres for about 140 metres before landing in a hedge. It was the first aircraft to use ailerons, instead of the inferior wing warping system that the Wright brothers used. By the end of that year Richard was doing flights of up to one kilometre and some of them included turns.

The sad thing about Richard was that people didn't understand him. They thought he was strange, possibly mad, and that his actions would bring disaster. Parents thrashed any children who watched him trying to make his planes fly. They believed that God never intended man to fly. So Richard had to work in secret. It took a lot of courage for him to continue.

In Numbers chapter 13 we read about how when the people

of Israel came to the Promised Land, Moses sent out twelve spies. Ten came back in terror, believing that disaster would hit them if they went on. Only two, Joshua and Caleb, had the courage to believe that this was God's land for them. Caleb said, 'We should go up and take possession of the land, for we can certainly do it,' (Numbers 13:30). Joshua and Caleb said: 'The land we passed through is exceedingly good. If the Lord is pleased with us He will lead us into that land, a land flowing with milk and honey and will give it to us. Only do not rebel against the Lord. And do not be afraid of the people of the land, because we will swallow them up. Their protection is gone, but the Lord is with us. Do not be afraid of them' (Numbers 14:7-9).

The people didn't listen to Joshua and Caleb so they had to spend another forty years wandering in the desert.

Sadly this often happens. But in Richard's case, many decades later, God used further developments in aviation to support missions in a wonderful way. It happened this way. During the Second World War a young New Zealander named Murray Kendon was flying with the RAF Coastal Command. He began to think about the way airplanes might help missionaries to reach remote people who didn't know Jesus and so bring hope to millions in isolated places. Together with some other people with the same vision, he started what became known as Missionary Aviation Fellowship. The first plane flew out in 1949 and since then it has become an international organisation which has made a huge difference to missions. It doesn't just help them to reach distant, otherwise inaccessible places, but also brings sick missionaries back to hospital and carries urgently needed supplies.

When ideas come to us we can test them and see if they come from God. We can do this by reading the Bible like the Bereans did: 'Day after day they studied the Scriptures to see if these things were true' (Acts 17:11). If we find that they are from God, then we need the courage to put them into action even if others criticise us.

Moeraki Boulders

Your adventure now takes you south to Dunedin, all the way hugging the beautiful rugged coastline. Soon after crossing a mile long bridge over the mighty Waitaki River, you arrive in the province of Otago.

Before long you will see a sign to 'Koekohe Beach', the only place in the world where you can see giant grey 'Moeraki Boulders'.

Moeraki Boulders are perfectly round and come in all sizes, from quite small, to twelve feet in circumference. According to Maori legend they have something to do with the loss of the Arai-te-uru, one of the large sailing canoes that brought the tribes from Hawaiki. On one of the rocks overlooking the beach stands what they believe to be the petrified body of the commander.

17

The boulders strewn all over the beach are the eel baskets, calabashes and sweet potatoes washed ashore from the wreck. Scientists, however, think it is more likely that the boulders have been formed by the sea. No one really knows.

Many years ago the campers at a Christian holiday camp went to the beach to see how many people could fit on a boulder. You can imagine how big the boulders are when I tell you that eighteen managed to squeeze on to it. When we handed up our one year old son it made nineteen!

After passing through the city of Oamaru you finally arrive in the fourth largest city of New Zealand, Dunedin. It is fourth in population but the largest city in land area.

Otago is an anglicised version of the Maori settlement of Otakou, a busy nineteenth century whaling base on the Otago Peninsula.

To understand how Dunedin started, we need to go back to Scotland. In the nineteenth century, at a time which was known as the Disruption in Scotland, evangelical Presbyterians left the established Church and started what they called the Free Church of Scotland. Many believed God called them to leave Scotland altogether. But where should they go? They dreamt of a Scottish community and a Free Church somewhere else.

It wasn't only the people who were upset by the church who wanted to leave Scotland. Because of the Highland Clearances, a lot of Scottish people lost their land, homes and work. They, too, wanted a new start somewhere else.

New Zealand sounded like a land of promise. Leaders of the Free Church enquired from the London base of the New Zealand Society and in 1844 Edward Gibbon Wakefield sent a man called Frederick Tuckett south to have a look at the Otago area as a possibility for a settlement. Tuckett hired some Maori guides who took him round the Otago Harbour, up the Clutha River, round Lake Waihola and the Taieri and Tokomairiro Plains. He recommended it as a good place, although during his tour he was often so cold that his boots froze.

In 1846 a surveyor called Charles Kettle went to have a look too. He was so sure it would work out that he bought what came to be known as the 'Otago Block' from the Maoris. He found that there was plenty of wood for fuel, fencing, building and land for pasture.

For the next two years surveyors and planners came in and laid out a city. Because it was to be a Scottish settlement, it was called Dunedin, the Gaelic equivalent of Edinburgh. Many of its streets have Edinburgh names.

The Lay Association of the Free Church of Scotland now chartered two ships and invited people willing to go to the new land to sign up. The *John Wickliffe* (with ninety-six passengers) and the *Philip Laing* (with 247 passengers) arrived in Dunedin in 1848. Apart from their personal belongings, they brought tools, muskets, slates, bricks and other building materials as well as school books. A minister, the Reverend Thomas Burns, and a school master, William Cargill, were also among the emigrants. As part of his luggage, the Reverend Burns brought a prefabricated house for his family.

The new settlers started building straightaway. But the first winter was wet and very cold and many would have died if it hadn't been for Johnny Jones, the whaler. During his whaling days, Johnny had thought about the future and set up a big farm just north of Dunedin. From this he was able to provide the settlers with fresh food.

In the book of Esther we read that Mordecai sent a message to his beautiful cousin Esther telling her that it might be 'for such a time as this' that she had been picked by the King for his bride. This might be the plan that God had to save his people, he told her. And it turned out to be just that.

It's not difficult to imagine that God had planned for Johnny Jones to set up a farm so that the Scottish Christians would have food to eat. When God gives you something to do, you can be sure that He has gone before and prepared the way so that you can complete the job, even though it may be difficult.

More ships came in 1848 and 1849 but some of the later new arrivals weren't from Scotland and were not in the least bit interested in living in a Free Church community. The hope that it would be a totally Presbyterian settlement faded somewhat. This was obvious when, on the anniversary of the first settlers arriving in Dunedin, there were two celebrations: one a service of thanksgiving, humiliation and prayer, and another for those who decided to enjoy a day of sport and fun instead.

The Reverend Thomas Burns was not just interested in looking

after the spiritual needs of the settlers. He also used his skills to help them build good homes and find ways to earn a livelihood. One of the ideas he had was to get each of them some land to buy. The way he did it was to set up an organisation he called the Otago-Southland Synod. He bought large blocks of land, and sold it on to the new settlers in lots. From the money they paid him he set aside one eighth of the money, for God's work.

This money has grown over the years and today it still funds many evangelistic projects in the Otago Southland region. It also helps to maintain some of the beautiful old churches built during the early days of settlement.

Jesus told a story about yeast. He said in Matthew 13:33 that even a small amount mixed into a large amount of flour goes all through it. It makes it grow. This is what the Synod did. The early settlers were faithful about giving their money to help with God's work. Giving a regular part of our money to God's work is what God expects from us too and He will bless us when we keep this command.

Otago was a quiet and refined settlement where the only policeman had nothing to do, until, in 1861, a man called Gabriel Read discovered gold in the Central part of the province and miners poured in from all over the world. This changed Dunedin into a bustling and wealthy city. Later on in this adventure you will visit the gold fields and learn more about what happened.

One good thing that came from the gold rush, however, was that the city fathers wisely used some of the wealth that came to the town to build churches and public buildings, including the first university in New Zealand.

The Royal Albatross

Find a friend about the same size as you and lie down with your feet meeting. That is about the wingspread of a royal albatross (three metres). It is the largest of the albatross family of birds.

To see a soaring royal albatross is something you never forget. It is not only huge, but it is capable of swooping speeds of more than 115 kilometres per hour. You can, if you are lucky, see one take off from Taiaroa Head, an open headland with wild gales blowing across it at the end of the Otago Peninsula. This is the only place in the world where the royal albatross breeds so close to human habitation.

In 1920, for the first time, a royal albatross egg was found at Taiaroa Head and it was clear that not only did the birds visit, it was a place they came to breed. But cats, dogs, ferrets, stoats and rabbits roamed free in the area and sometimes there were fires which threatened to destroy the vegetation. Even the egg was stolen. The colony was in dire peril. Yet it wasn't until 1937 that the Taiaroa Head nesting place became protected. A fence was built around it and, in 1951, a full time field officer appointed to look after it. A visitor viewing place now protects the birds from threatening human curiosity. All the birds and their chicks are banded and carefully monitored and because of this a lot is now known about the life of the royal albatross. There are now more than 130 birds in its population.

The royal albatross generally lives on the oceans of the world and only comes to land to breed. It eats mostly sea eggs (a type of sea urchin), fish, fish eggs and squid, drinks salt water and sleeps on the waves. The royal albatross lives a long time – one bird is known to have raised her last chick when she was sixty-two years old!

Albatross generally don't flap their wings – they understand the patterns of the wind and use them for what is known as dynamic soaring and slope soaring. Dynamic soaring enables them to minimise the effort needed by gliding across wave fronts gaining energy from the vertical wind gradient. Slope soaring is more straightforward: the albatross turns into the wind to gain height, and then glides back down to the sea. It needs wind to fly, so if it hits calm seas, it rests on the surface of the ocean until the wind picks up again. This is the reason that sailors are happy to see an albatross in flight because they know that there are good winds on the way!

The royal albatross doesn't think about starting a family until he is about eight years old. That's when he returns to Taiaroa in September to find his mate and build a nest. They seem to know exactly where they were born themselves and build within a short distance of their own hatching site.

In November the female lays just one egg, which is the height of a can of coca-cola and weighs about 500 grams. The parents take turns sitting on the egg for about eleven weeks until it is ready to hatch. From the first tiny hole in the egg, it takes about six days for a little chick to appear in the nest. The parents guard and feed their baby for about forty days. That's the time when they know the chick can protect itself from predators and it is safe for them to leave it for longer periods.

The growing chicks have a great social life with parties, courtships and finally matching up with a mate for life.

When they are about forty weeks old, something tells them that it's time to take off. Unlike many birds, they don't get any flying lessons from their parents, they just know what to do.

For a few days they test their wings on the 'runway' and then, when they feel the right wind they take off. When the parents return to find their chick gone they too know they are free to roam the wide oceans again. Their job is done and they can return to what they love best.

There is a time when our parents look after us. Hopefully they will teach us to follow Jesus but there is also a time when we must make a decision to follow Jesus. Just as the albatross chick decides to leave the nest, so we have to decide to follow Jesus. No one else can make that decision for us.

St Augustine prayed to God once 'Our hearts are restless until they find their rest in Thee.' Just like the royal albatross, who is never happier than when he is soaring on the wind over the wild oceans of the world, you cannot be really happy if you are not walking on the path God has specially designed for you. You must rest in the Lord God - trust in him and follow his ways.

The Bird that Shouts

In 1973 a man called John Darby set out to study the yellow eye penguin. Their numbers had been getting so low that they might disappear altogether. John Darby wanted to make sure that didn't happen.

The yellow eye penguin is the fourth largest of the seventeen kinds of penguins in the world. The largest is the emperor penguin (about 30 kilograms) and the smallest is the little blue penguin (just over 1 kilogram). The yellow eye weighs about 5 kilograms. It gets its name from the distinctive yellow band around its head. The Maori name for the yellow eyed penguin is Hoiho - 'The bird that shouts' - because of its loud cry.

All penguins live in the southern hemisphere but the yellow eye is unique to the East Coast of the south island of New Zealand

and some islands further south. It once lived in the forests by the sea, but many of these forests were cut down for timber, or burnt down to make farmland. So now they live among the flax bushes which grow on the hill sides.

John Darby put little steel bands with special numbers on all the yellow eye chicks he could find. Twenty years later he made a graph about what he had discovered. He found that some of the first penguins he had banded were still alive!

But he also made a sad discovery. All the chicks banded that year had died – he found them with ferret bites on the back of their head. It wasn't difficult to work out who was to blame!

In 1990 he made another discovery. This time it wasn't just the chicks that had died, but a lot of adults as well. He decided a mystery disease must have killed them.

John now decided the time had come to do a census of all the yellow eyes so that he could get a picture of just how many there were left. In 1990 and 1992 he travelled down the entire coast of the South Island and finally came up with a tally of somewhere between 1,200 and 1,500 pairs. Then he knew for sure that the yellow eye was the rarest penguin in the world.

Now that it was clear that the yellow eye penguin might die out, people began to look out for ways to help them.

One such person was farmer Howard McGrouther, who, in 1984, built Penguin Place, not far away from the Dunedin Albatross Colony. Mr McGrouther had been farming there since 1958 and often watched the penguins on the beach at the edge of his farm. He was concerned that they were going down in numbers. In 1984 he counted just eight breeding pairs! So what could he do?

He knew that ferrets, stoats and cats killed penguin chicks so he built a protective fence round his farm and set traps for the predators. He also planted flaxes for the penguins to nest in.

Then he thought it might be a good idea to build a place where people could watch the penguins and learn about them. To begin with he set up a rehabilitation centre on his property to care for sick or injured penguins. Then he built some camouflaged tunnels for observers. He called it Penguin Place and twenty years after he first began counting the total was twenty-one breeding pairs.

One windy day we took three of our grandchildren to visit Penguin Place. After a talk about the Yellow Eye a bus took us over rough farming country to the starting place of the tour. As soon as we got off the bus, a guide took us into the network of tunnels with windows at eye level, so we could see out, but the penguins, who are people-shy, wouldn't be disturbed.

Within a few minutes we saw our first penguin, just metres from our window. He was clearly moulting. Yellow-eye penguins moult around February. They lose their old feather coat and a new one grows from underneath. Until it is complete it is too cold for them to go fishing and as none of their friends help them, they get very hungry and thin. All day long, he just stands there, waiting for the moment when he can go swimming again.

It is a very special thing to see a moulting penguin. In the Book of Matthew, Jesus warned his friends not to worry: 'I tell you not to worry about your life. Don't worry about having something to eat, drink, or wear. Isn't life more than food or clothing? Look at the birds in the sky! They don't plant or harvest. They don't even store grain in barns. Yet your Father in heaven takes care of them. Aren't you worth much more than the birds? Can worry make you live longer? Why worry about clothes? Look how the wild flowers grow. They don't work hard to make their clothes. But I tell you that Solomon with all his wealth wasn't as well clothed as one of them. God gives such beauty to everything that grows in the fields, even though it is here today and thrown into a fire tomorrow. He will surely do even more for you? Why do you have so little faith?' (Matthew 6:25-30).

The moulting yellow eye didn't know what would happen, but something inside him told him that he must just stand and wait. He couldn't fish for food but he is made to be able to last just long enough without it. And soon his sparkling new white coat is more magnificent than anything a king might wear.

When things are hard for you think about the penguin and what Jesus said. Put your trust in God and it will work out.

We knew that some penguins hadn't starting moulting and

others had finished. From the tunnel windows we could see the beach. We stood very still and watched. It was late afternoon and about time for the penguins to come in from their day's swimming. Everyone was very quiet.

"There's one," someone whispered. And so there was. Soon more penguins swam in on the big waves, stood up, shook themselves and looked around. Before long the small beach was quite crowded. It seemed like a party. We were too far away to hear what they said, but it looked as though this was their social hour, when everyone shared their adventures of the day; how far they might have gone, whether they had found plenty of small fish and krill, how deep they might have had to dive to get them (they can go as far down as 120 metres) and whether they had seen any killer whales.

Soon it was time for them to waddle up the narrow paths to their nests among the flax bushes and rest until the next morning.

Shipwrecks and Sea Lions

In the summer of 1993, on a beautiful sandy beach, just south of Dunedin, a hooker's sea lion gave birth to a pup. She was the first sea lion to do that in 400 years. The people in the village of Taieri Mouth watched amazed as she tended her baby only to disappear with the pup a few weeks later. The pair had gone to Victory Beach, not far from Penguin Place. Since then, she has come every year to Taieri Mouth to have her babies, always moving on to Victory Beach soon after.

In 2007 the few residents of the community, who had come to love the sea lion they called 'Mum' were concerned when they found the latest pup on the beach but no sign of its mother. They knew sea lions can't live off what they find on the beach;

sooner or later they have to go 'shopping' for food on the ocean floor. So at first no one worried. But when the pup started to look hungry and sick they wondered if its mother had perhaps got caught in a net and died. They did their best to care for her pup. Two weeks later, Mum returned, looking the worse for wear, and too late to save her baby.

Not far south of Taieri Mouth is the Catlins Coast where you can see a whole beach full of male hooker sea lions. The Catlins is a wild and wonderful place, unique with its wildlife and spectacular natural places. Its dense forests, towering cliffs, rocky coastal bays, inlets and estuaries are home to many birds and large mammals lost from more populated places.

The small seaside resort of Kaka Point is a great place to start exploring the Catlins. Once the home base of a busy fishing fleet, fresh cod is on the menu in its only restaurant. Not far away is the Nuggets Lighthouse, so named because it sits above the rocks, nicknamed 'the nuggets', that surround the point.

Many of the early ships bringing settlers for Dunedin sailed round the Cape of Good Hope. Their first sighting of the country they had come to was the southern Solander Island, then they sailed past Stewart Island to reach the rocky point guarding the harbour. But at that time many ships were driven on to the wild east coast of the south island by the fierce winds coming off the southern ocean. Clearly a lighthouse was needed to warn the sailors of the dangers.

The Nugget Lighthouse began to send out its beam in 1870. As you climb up the steep hill to it you may see New Zealand sea lions, New Zealand fur seals, and elephant seals lazing in the bays far down below you. Many species of sea birds also nest in the rocks below. It is one of the few places in New Zealand where the huge, deep-diving elephant seal nests.

Three kinds of sea lions regularly visit the Catlins. The first is the hooker's sea lion. These sea lions mainly breed around New

Zealand's subantarctic islands, especially Enderby and Dundas Island which is only the size of two football fields.

As sea lions love to eat squid, every year many sea lions die in the huge squid nets used by fishing fleets. Since trawl fishing began in 1978, more than 2,000 sea lions have died in this way. To protect them from certain extinction, the New Zealand Government has set a limit on how many sea lions the squid fishermen can catch before they have to stop fishing.

The hooker's sea lion is the rarest sea lion in the world. In the early nineteenth century they were hunted for food and their pelts. By 1998, there were only somewhere between 11,000 and 15,000 of these animals in the world. That year they were struck by a disastrous illness which killed about 20 per cent of the adults and 50 per cent of the pups born that year.

The New Zealand fur seal isn't actually a seal at all. True seals have a little ear hole in the sides of their head, their feet are fused together and they have to use their whole body to move about on land. The New Zealand fur seal is related to the hooker's sea lion. Like the hooker it has external ear flaps and limbs it can walk on but they are smaller in size.

The elephant seal is the most difficult to find. He is a very large seal – the largest known measured 6.7 metres in length and weighed 3,400 kilograms (nearly 4 tons). It spends most of its time in the ocean and can hold its breath for over eighty minutes. It can dive to 1,500 metres below the sea surface. Elephant seals come ashore from time to time if they are sick, when they are ready to moult or just for a rest.

Not far from Kaka Point is the small village of Pounawea, well known for its Christian convention centre. Each year Christians come here from all over southern New Zealand for a time of fellowship and learning about Jesus.

Just up the road is Surat Bay, so called because on New Year's Day, 1874, a ship called 'The Surat', carrying new settlers, was

wrecked there. Fortunately none of the passengers were lost. As you walk along the beach you will see many 'logs', which, as you get close to them, are actually hooker's sea lions. It is one of the few places in the world where these very rare, huge animals nest. There are warnings everywhere about not getting too close to them, as they have been known to attack humans.

Taieri's sea lion, Mum, and the settlers who came on the 'Surat' have something in common. They are all pioneers. Mum came to New Zealand when none of her kind had been seen there for 400 years. The settlers were going to Dunedin, believing that God had called them to a new country. That took a lot of courage. In

the book of Joshua we learn how the children of Israel came to a new country which God had given them. But before they could live there, there were many battles to be won. That took courage and faith. They had already turned away once before because they were too frightened. Now God spoke to their leader, Joshua. 'I've commanded you to be strong and brave,' He said. 'Don't ever be afraid or discouraged! I am the Lord your God and I will be there to help you wherever you go.' Do you have to start something new sometimes and you are frightened about whether you can do it? Whether you will find new friends or where you will live? Then you can take God's promise to Joshua for your own. But you will need to have courage and faith and listen to God's commands along the way: 'Never stop reading the Book of the Law. Day and night you must think about what it says. If you obey it completely, you and Israel will be able to take this land.'

One day we planned to walk along the dunes of Surat Bay when we spotted a family who were just coming back. The father and the children were not far from us, but the mother was quite a way behind them. As we watched, two huge sea lions landed on the beach between the walkers.

The mother stood absolutely still. The sea lions waddled to an edge of a dune where, peeping out from under some flax bushes we now saw a third sea lion, a baby! The older two greeted the baby enthusiastically and the three cuddled and kissed each other. They were clearly a family. This was a very unusual thing for human beings to see.

If the sea lions had spotted the woman her life might well have been in danger. There was no way she could escape! She just had to wait until they returned to the water or lay down in the sun and went to sleep. Then taking care not to disturb them, she could join her family. What a story they had to tell when they were all safely together again!

Hoppers and Jumpers

A few kilometres south of Surat Bay is the Lenz Reserve. Walking through indigenous trees and shrubs around a small lake, you will see New Zealand native wood pigeons and, if you come in summer, the Rata trees will be in flower. In the north island, the Pohutukawa tree with its red flowers has become known as the New Zealand Christmas tree. The Rata is the southern version of it.

In New Zealand we celebrate Christmas in summer, which isn't very easy if you are used to winter at that time. In the early days new settlers from the northern hemisphere, where it snows at Christmas, tried to celebrate Christmas in their traditional way. But with a hot sun shining outside that didn't work too well and with the years they adapted to a new style of enjoying the Festival. Instead of turkeys, they chose spring lamb, new potatoes, fresh peas and salads. Today many people stay outside in the sunshine and enjoy a barbecue dinner. Instead of the traditional plum duff they have a special dessert known as Pavlova, a meringue cake with a marshmellow centre, topped with fresh strawberries and lashings of cream. It was created in New Zealand in the 1920s and named after the Russian ballerina Anna Pavlova. Just before their Christmas dinner or late into the evening many New Zealanders go swimming in one of the many lakes, rivers or, if they are near a beach, the sea!

From the Lenz Reserve a long board walk will take you through the Tautuku River Estuary. Here you can sometimes see a South Island fern bird. This rare little brown spotted bird is a ground dweller that loves the estuary's salt marshes. They don't fly well and when they do, it's with their tails down. Because they are such weak fliers they are very vulnerable if there is a fire in their habitat. Some people come from far away countries just to see the fern bird. It is almost unbelievable that you can walk so far out into this lovely wetland of beautiful grasses and rushes surrounded by native forest.

There are two interesting things about the fern bird. The first is that both parents work together to build their nest and look after their beautiful, tiny eggs – a delicate translucent pink, with tiny brown spots, until their chicks are hatched and have learnt to fly.

The other is that one of their favourite perches is the back of a fur seal or sea lion where they catch the flies which so irritate and annoy it. These huge mammals greatly appreciate the hard work of the little bird. It reminds me of a person in the Bible. In Colossians 4:7-8 and other letters from Paul we read about a man with a servant heart. We read: 'Tychicus will tell you all the news about me. He is a dear brother, a faithful minister and fellow servant in the Lord.' We don't know much about Tychicus, but he was happy to serve Paul in any way he could and Paul could rely

on him to do a job well. God gives each of us gifts to use for him: some to become leaders, but most of us to be servants. What matters is that we use the gifts God has given us and not look jealously at others who are more important than we are. Tychicus could be trusted and did things well. The job of catching flies is not very important in the eyes of the world, but it makes a huge difference to the sea lion.

We can't leave the Catlins without seeing Curio Bay, also known as Porpoise Bay. This name is curious because there are no porpoises there – but hector's dolphins are of the same family and it is hector's dolphins you will see jumping high and out of the water and playing joyfully with each other around the high waves that roll into the beach. Amazingly they seem to enjoy human company and play around the surf riders who are often found there.

The hector's dolphin is the most threatened kind of dolphin in the world and even in Curio Bay there aren't as many as there used to be. Those who study the dolphins think that this is because some of the tourists who visit the bay don't know how to behave around dolphins and put them off. They love to go into the water and swim with the dolphins, but get too close to them. For a number of years government rangers have tried to work out how many hector's dolphins actually visit the southern coast of New Zealand. They use a curious method for this. Rather than tag the ones they find, they photograph the dolphin's dorsal fins, which usually have unusual marks that allow them to be recognized. One dolphin, for instance, has a sharp step notched out of its fin and is known as 'Step'. Others have propeller scars from boats. Once the rangers get a feel for where the dolphins go, they can try and work out what is threatening them.

The southernmost point of the South Island is Slope Point which also marks the end of the Catlins. This beach was the place where one of the worst shipping disasters happened. In

1881, the ship 'Tararua' was wrecked off the reef, just offshore and 131 people died. There is no sign of the wreck today. The Waipapa Point Lighthouse above the beach is all locked up too. But if you take the path from the lighthouse to the beach you need to be very careful not to step on a sea lion. Usually there are many of them hauled out on the rocks. They are not too keen on photographers and have been known to playfully chase them away!

Jet-setters of the Bird World

We are used to long distance flying these days, but would you believe that there are birds that clock up 65,000 kilometres on their annual migration from the southern to the northern hemisphere, and back each year?

The sooty shearwater has a sooty colour and skimming flight pattern. Its major breeding grounds are on the remote islands off southern New Zealand, especially Mana and Codfish Island.

It is about the size of a duck and is commonly known as mutton bird. Although they don't look like sheep they do taste like the sheep meat which is called mutton. Mutton birds are still a popular food, especially with the Maori people, and hundreds of thousands are harvested each year.

The mutton bird lays just one egg each year and parents take it in turn to hatch it. But once the chick is born, its parents leave it in the nest while both of them go hunting for food. They may leave it for ten days at a time. You'd have thought that when they come back they would hurry to their nest, but they don't. They land on the water off the island and rest on the waves till other returning parents arrive. When everyone seems to be there, they all take off from the sea together, circle the area a few times and land near their nests. Then they feed their babies with a rich oil – the hungry chicks may eat twice their own weight in a short time. As soon as they feel the chick can manage on its own, the parents set out on their long journey to the northern hemisphere.

Once their parents have left, the young birds have nothing more to eat and lose a lot of weight. But their flight feathers are growing vigorously. They venture outside the burrow each day, gradually moving closer to the beach and testing their wings. Two or three weeks after their parents have left, the young birds begin their own migratory flight without their parents. A tiny in built 'computer' programmes their long and lonely journey.

Not a lot was known about the migratory patterns because during their time in the north they stay on the water and don't make landfall. Sometimes exhausted and starved birds washed ashore on the beaches of Japan, the Aleutian Islands, and North America provided a clue as to their whereabouts.

Early in 2005, a team of scientists from New Zealand, the USA and France, put 'geolocator' electronic tags on some of the birds and followed their migration from breeding colonies on Mana and Codfish Island. These tags allowed the scientists to track their progress on a daily basis. To their amazement they learnt that the birds traversed the Pacific in figure of eight patterns for about 200 days, pursuing an endless summer of good food. Some birds flew up to 910 kilometres in a single day.

They returned in October, when they were no longer hungry and all crossed the equator within a five day period. One scientist, a sea bird biologist, said that this was the longest and most unusual animal migration recorded via an electronic tracking device.

The brain of the mutton bird is no bigger than the top of your thumb, but God has programmed it to make its amazing journey with unerring accuracy. In a way, God has programmed us too. If we obey him we will live a life that brings glory to His name. In Psalm 139 King David wrote: 'You are the one who put me together inside my mother's body, and I praise you because of the wonderful way you created me. Everything you do is marvellous!' (Psalm 139: 13-14)

But, unlike the mutton bird, we can choose whether we do what God planned for us. King David prayed that God would help him to choose His ways and keep him from doing wrong. 'Look into my heart, God,' he wrote 'and find out everything I am thinking. Don't let me follow evil ways but lead me in the way that time has proven true,' (Psalm 139: 23-24).

You would enjoy reading all of Psalm 139 now. It is only when we follow God's plan for our lives that we will be happy. But we need to be looking for it by reading the Bible and listening for His voice as we pray.

The islands where the mutton birds nest are not open to ordinary people, but nearby Stewart Island welcomes visitors. On most days there are three or four sailings from Bluff at the southern tip of the South Island. It is a busy port. Paper products from the Mataura paper mills, just north of Invercargill, and frozen meat have long been shipped to England from Bluff.

A one hour journey across Foveaux Straight takes people to Stewart Island. About halfway you will pass the island of Ruapuke, now mostly deserted, but it once was a whaling base and the largest Maori settlement in southern New Zealand. It was also the home of Tuhawaiki, King of the Bluff and the paramount chief of the South Island.

In the mid nineteenth century a missionary came to Ruapuke. The Reverend Johann Wohlers was sent to New Zealand by a

German missionary society which had a base in Nelson, at the top of the south island. But after a sad dispute over land between the would-be settlers and the local Maori the German missionaries decided to go elsewhere. Travelling with Fred Tuckett who was looking for a place for a proposed Scottish settlement (Dunedin) they visited Ruapuke Island where Wohlers decided to stay and establish a mission base.

The Ruapuke Maori people were a very primitive civilisation, desperately poor and without hope. Wohlers had grown up on a farm in northern Germany so he knew how to survive from the land. He set about improving their lives, teaching them how to grow vegetables and wheat, introducing them to sheep and cattle. He became fluent in the Maori language and started a school for the children. After five lonely years on Ruapuke, God gave him a wife, a wonderful Christian lady called Eliza Palmer. She was a wonderful help to him, training girls in housework and teaching the people ways to care for the sick. Together they brought many to faith in Christ

When God gives us a calling we must obey him too. We may not want to do it and it can be difficult but if we obey we will be blessed. In the Bible we read that Noah had to build an ark when there was no water anywhere near to sail it. All his neighbours made fun of him. Jeremiah was sent to give bad news to people who didn't want to hear about it. Wohlers had to leave his home to go to a distant island where he didn't know anyone. In 1 Corinthians chapter 4 we read about how Paul was given the work of explaining God's mysterious ways. Paul said it was our duty to be faithful to God, the one we work for. In verse five we find a promise: 'Then God will be the one who praises each of us.' Who knows what God will ask you to do with your life? Whatever it is, to obtain a blessing you must obey.

Stewart Island is one of the few places in New Zealand where you can actually see a brown kiwi in the wild. In general, the five species of kiwi are nocturnal; the brown kiwi is the only one that comes out during the day. Most people who are willing to hike long distances or take a boat round the wild coastline, will see one, often in the early evening when the birds fossick along the edge of the forest.

Watch Out for Parrots

A short water taxi ride across Stewart Island's Paterson Inlet will take you to Ulva Island which has been cleared of predators. As you land you will be greeted by weka wandering on the beach. Along the island's clearly marked paths you can look for oyster catchers, Stewart Island robins, tui, bellbirds, kakas, grey warblers, and, if you are very lucky, a shining cuckoo, saddlebacks, parakeets (both red and yellow crowned), wood pigeons which love to eat the brilliant red berries of the miro tree and, of course, the cheeky fantails which may even land on your head.

Much of the south western part of the South Island is a World

Heritage area and the Fiordland National Park is an important part of it.

It is a wild, rugged country where few humans have ever been. There are jagged, razor backed mountains, granite precipices and even active earthquake faults.

As it rains there for about 200 days every year the forests are intensely green and thick. Deep fiords penetrate the mountain ranges and provide safe havens for all types of wild life, including the green parrot of the night, the kakapo.

The kakapo is the biggest and most unusual parrot in the world. It weighs up to 4 kilograms and can't fly. In the days of the early settlers in New Zealand it was found up and down New Zealand. People loved the friendly bird clowns, whose clever acrobatics, games with various props, provided endless entertainment. Some even kept them as pets.

In its natural habitat, the kakapo is very strong and it climbs into the crowns of tall trees to collect its fruit. It likes its own company and in a night might travel several kilometers to find food. It eats grass, fruit from forest trees, parts of plants (roots, rhizomes, bulbs, twigs, buds, leaves, leaf stems, flowers, flower stems, pollen cones, fruits, berries, seeds and bark).

Because it has a down layer beneath its moss and leaf green

speckled feathers, the kakapo can live in cold climates. He keeps these feathers in good condition by grooming them with oil from a gland above its tail. Used as camouflage, they are his main defence, but they don't protect him from his chief enemy, wild cats, who go by smell. Early Maori hunted the kakapo for its meat and used its feathers for their cloaks.

The kakapo is best known for his unusual way of attracting females in the breeding season. The male bird makes a special track (as much as 50 metres in length) which leads to a 'bowl', about 5 centimetres deep and 45 centimetres wide. This bowl acts like a sound shell. At night he stands in the middle of his bowl, inflates the air sacs in his chest and 'booms' - so loudly that it can be heard up to five kilometers away. This continues from dusk till dawn. It is known as a 'lek' mating system.

Around 1900 it became clear to everyone that wild cats, stoats, ferrets, weasels and dogs were killing too many kakapo and their numbers had dwindled alarmingly. In fact, in most of New Zealand they had disappeared altogether.

The government then decided to try and catch some of them and move them to safer places where they could be protected. This proved to be very expensive and with two world wars and an economic depression in the 1930s, the project got lost.

By 1945 it was thought that there were fewer than one hundred kakapo left and soon they would be gone altogether. The New Zealand Wildlife Service set up expeditions to find out what the situation was. They found them in Fiordland, and to their surprise, in Stewart Island. This was especially exciting, because there, for the first time, they found some females.

With the situation now so critical, the New Zealand Wild Life Service set up a Kakapo Recovery Programme to save the species. They eventually caught about sixty kakapo and transferred them to two predator free islands. By 2005, after many set-backs, this number had grown to ninety.

For more than a century many people gave huge amounts of time and money to save one bird species. But think of what God has given to save you and me! The Bible says: 'God loved the world so much that He gave His only Son, so that everyone who has faith in Him will have eternal life and never really die. God did not send his Son into the world to condemn its people. He sent him to save them. No one who has faith in God's son will be condemned.' (John 3:16 TEV)

God loved his Son utterly and completely, as only God can, and yet He sent Him to save you and me. All you have to do is accept God's gift – it is free for the asking!

Kakapo numbers continue to rise, but its survival is still by no means certain and it may not be possible to ever return them to the places where they used to live.

Lake Manapouri and Doubtful Sound are two parts of the national park and it is in this area that we see an example of human beings and nature co-existing together. There is a large hydro-electric scheme in this area which has been generating power for the community since the 1960s. It is wonderful to journey on the Sound at night. It may be raining hard when you go out, but in the morning the mists rise slowly above the water and gradually reveal the mountains – higher and higher. Dolphins often swim alongside your ship,

Amazingly, the Sound has two layers of water – the top few

metres are fresh water, fed from the steep mountains above it, below is salt water. Because light does not easily penetrate to this layer, some deep sea species such as black coral can grow here. Star fish and many other kinds of fish, sea anemones and other corals grow here in abundance.

What a marvellous world God has created for us! King David said, 'I know every bird in the mountains, and the creatures of the field are mine' (Psalm 50:11 NIV). It is not surprising that when we see all these miracles of nature, our hearts turn to God.

Lake Te Anau Mysteries

Just a few kilometres from Manapouri is New Zealand's second largest lake, Te Anau. Its original Maori name was Te Anau-au, which means 'cave with a current of swirling waters'.

As a young man, Lawson Burrows heard a legend about Lake Te Anau. The story told how Te Horo, a Maori Chief, discovered a cave with a sacred spring and asked his wife not to tell anyone about it. But she did and when Te Horo found out he was so angry that a wild, swirling torrent burst loose from the spring, drowned the whole village and made a huge lake. It is known as Lake Te Anau.

Lawson Burrows was fascinated by this legend and wondered if perhaps there was a grain of truth in it. He decided to look for the lost cave and the underground stream flowing from it. For three years he searched the 300 miles of lakeshore, but he didn't find them.

Then, in 1948, his eye was drawn to a small stream disappearing into the hillside under a buttress of rock. Could this be what he was looking for?

He dived into the water, pushed himself through the entrance and found himself in a magic world of twinkling lights - glow-worms! 'It was a fantastic sight,' he said later. 'It looked like a page out of a science fiction book, a weird place, but not at all frightening.' He was convinced he had found what he was looking for.

Have you ever seen glow-worms? They are the larvae of fungus gnats, small flies with a four part life cycle: egg, larvae, pupae and adult fly.

Their actual 'glow' is the oxidisation of a chemical called luciferin present inside the glow worm's digestive tract. The glow worm light shines as a blue/green colour and the hungrier the glow worm is the more brightly it glows.

Flying insects are attracted by large numbers of lights in the dark cave that mimic the night sky. The glow worms send sticky silk threads down from their nests to capture the insects and haul them back, like a fisherman bringing in his line. They can turn their light on and off when they are disturbed by unusual noises, light, humidity and temperature. Its intensity varies with their desire for food.

After his discovery, Lawson Burrows set up a business taking people to see the glow worms. A thirty five minute boat trip will take you across Lake Te Anau to land on a purpose built wharf. Then a special cave vessel will take you into the caves beyond the roar of the stream into the 'cavern of silence', the glow-worm grotto. You have to be very quiet and not use torches or you will disturb the glow-worms. But you soon get used to the dark and enjoy the tiny lights all around you. The way out is along a special board walk through the limestone caverns.

Above the caves are the Murchison Mountains, the scene of another mystery.

In the 1930s a young Invercargill boy, Geoffrey Orbell, saw

a photo of a stuffed takahe, a large New Zealand native bird believed to be extinct. Geoffrey was fascinated by the picture and often went back to look at it. When he grew up, he became a doctor but whenever he could get away, he went hunting in the Murchison Mountains. Always in the back of his mind was the hope that one day he might see a real takahe. We need to go back a little in time to understand what happened.

In the mid nineteenth century Walter Mantell, an amateur British naturalist and geologist moved to New Zealand to look for geological specimens for his father, Gideon Mantell, also a geologist.

In 1847 Walter came across a site where some bird bones had been discovered. He recognised some of the bones, but there was a perfect skull he couldn't identify. He packed it all up and sent the parcel to his father in London. His father was so fascinated he took the bones to Professor Richard Owen, a bird specialist. Professor Owen studied the skull and decided it was rather like that of a large swamp hen, and so a member of the rail family. He gave it a name: notornis (southern bird) and mantelli (in honour of its finder). In New Zealand it is known by its Maori name: takahe. It is the largest and the only flightless rail type bird in the world.

In fact, in Walter's time, there were quite a lot of takahe in New Zealand but they lived in the mountainous and more inaccessible parts of the country and weren't easy to find. One day, Walter came across some sealers who were about to cook a bird their dog had caught. He recognised it at once. It was a takahe! The sealers were hungry and weren't about to give him their dinner, but they were willing to sell the skin to him. Walter bought it and sent it to his dad who had it stuffed and put in a glass case. Over the next fifty years three more takahe were found and their remains preserved. But that was all, and everyone thought the bird was extinct. But then, in the 1940s some hunters found signs of a 'large bird' in Fiordland. They were sure it was a takahe and people began to get excited about it again. And that's where Geoffrey Orbell came into the story.

The picture he had seen kept coming back to his mind and when he heard that there might still be some takahe in the forest he took every opportunity to go looking for them. He never missed a chance to ask hunters if they had perhaps come across a large blue-green bird with a broad red beak.

One day, as he and some friends stood beside a lake, high in the Murchison Mountains, they heard a strange call. There were some strange tracks near the lake too. Could they be the tracks of a takahe? Geoffrey carefully measured them and drew pictures. When he got home he showed it to the bird experts. They couldn't tell him what they were, but didn't believe they could be from a takahe. 'That bird is extinct' they told him.

But Geoffrey wasn't about to give up. In November 1948 he and his friends decided to go back to that place. Suddenly, out from the snow tussock, stepped a large blue-green bird. It was a takake! A real live one! They hid in the grass and watched. This time Geoffrey had a camera and was able to photograph the bird that hadn't been seen for fifty years.

Now that the evidence was there, people started looking for more takahe. It became clear that the only place they could still be found was Fiordland and estimated there might be about 200 of them. It was worth trying to save them. It turned out to be quite a job!

In 1959 an amateur ornithologist, Elwyn Welch, a wildlife officer and a photographer went into the Murchison Mountains to search for takahe chicks and eggs. Elwyn had set up part of his North Island Wairarapa farm (Mount Bruce) to take care of any chicks they might find. For two years he had trained bantams to sit on eggs, even when put in boxes being moved around on the back of a truck or carried around in a backpack.

In November Elwyn drove his Austin A40 car with boxes, bantams and other gear, across Cook Strait to the South Island and on to Te Anau where he met up with the wildlife officer and photographer. Carrying their packs and boxes, they crossed Lake Te Anau and climbed into the valley where some takahe had been seen. This operation was highly secret and was called 'Operation Password'.

At first they didn't find any takahe, but while stopping briefly for lunch, biologist Peter Morrison felt something moving under the tussock grass they were sitting on. Gently pushing back the tussocks they discovered two takahe chicks! Elwyn wrapped them in his sweater and hurried down the hill to put them into a box with their new foster mothers. They didn't find any eggs.

The team returned to the lake, now called Lake Orbell, several times and eventually found some eggs. On Christmas day, 1972, the first chicks emerged from eggs laid by captive birds at Mount Bruce Native Bird Reserve. The problem at first was that the hatched chicks thought they were bantams and would not breed. It was finally decided to make a model takahe to sit on the eggs and feed the chicks using a takahe hand puppet. It worked!

Some of the research done by the group at Mount Bruce was later used with other conservation projects.

The next challenge was to return the takahe to its natural habitat as well as to some of the predator free islands off the coast of the South Island. This project has also been a success. Today there are about 170 takahe in Fiordland and about thirty on the islands.

Not far from the Te Anau township is a hiking track, built in the late 1980s. One day some hikers saw a takahe along the track. From his tag they knew he had been released two years earlier in the Murchison Mountains and must have wandered all the way round the lake to this side of the mountains.

Lawson Burrows and Geoffrey Orbell were men with a vision, which drove them to persist when no one believed them. In the Bible we

meet a man who stuck with a vision. God gave Moses a vision to lead the people of Israel to freedom in a land of their own, Canaan. 'I have seen how my people are suffering as slaves in Egypt, and I have heard them beg for my help because of the way they are mistreated...I will bring my people out of Egypt where there is good land, rich with milk and honey...I am sending you to lead my people…'(Exodus 3:7-10, CEV). At first, Moses thought he wasn't clever enough to do this job. But finally he knew he had to obey. For many years he followed God and led his people through the desert. And although he never actually got to live in the Promised Land, God took him up a mountain where he could see it.

God gives all of us challenges and commands He expects us to obey. For some it may be to go to a foreign country to tell others about Jesus, for others it may be to train in a special way or, when you are young, to make friends with someone no one likes. Keeping our vision bright and obeying God is the way to be happy.

High Country Sheep Station

New Zealand was always going to be a good place for sheep farming and the government encouraged immigrants to lease land and develop pastures. The early farmers brought sheep from Australia and Scotland and shipped the wool back to Britain.

At first they only exported the wool, but, after many years of research, in 1882 the first refrigerated ship, laden with sheep meat, left New Zealand for England. Before long, the meat was in shops throughout Britain! Since then the industry has grown and exports meat all over the world from New Zealand.

High country farms (also known as sheep stations) are huge in area, because the harsh environment can support only a few sheep per acre. One such farm is Aspiring Station, at the border of Mount Aspiring National Park, named after its highest peak, the beautiful Mount Aspiring. Travelling north from Te Anau, over the rugged, rocky and winding Crown Range, the highest national highway in the country, you will arrive in Wanaka, a small town beside the sparkling blue waters of Lake Wanaka. At the head of the lake are the snow capped mountains of the Great Divide – the mountains of the Southern Alps which divide the Western and Eastern parts of the South Island.

One of the great rivers flowing into Lake Wanaka from the high glaciers of the Aspiring plateau is the Matukituki River. Along this river are several sheep stations. Near the junction of the East and West Matukituki rivers is Mount Aspiring Station, established by John Aspinall.

John came to New Zealand in 1909 and worked as a cook at several remote sheep stations. During the first World War, along with many other young New Zealanders, he joined the army and fought in Egypt and France.

While on leave in England he met and married Amy Page. He shared with her his vision of establishing a high country farm when the war was over. Amy had never been anywhere but Liverpool so to come to the remote Matukituki Valley was a huge step. But she rose to the challenge. The couple moved into an old house left over from a saw mill which had long closed. It burnt down three months later and the young couple lost all their possessions including their wedding presents. Nine months later they had built a new house and were constructing farm yards and outbuildings.

It was a hard life – with long hard winters, rabbits causing troubles and keas attacking their sheep. The keas played games – landing on a sheep's back, screeching loudly and frightening them so they fell over bluffs. One of their tricks was to use their long curved beaks to peck large wounds in a sheep's back. This would get infected and causing blood poisoning which killed the sheep. Today sheep can be inoculated against blood poisoning and they survive.

The keas weren't all trouble, though. They were often good for a laugh as well. The only alpine parrot in the world, they are known for their inquisitive nature. They love to go round car parks, sliding down windscreens, pulling on wipers, hooking on to half open windows and pecking at tyre rims and valves. When trampers pitch camp, they have to be prepared for keas coming early in the morning or late at night and poking round their food supply or their belongings. Often called the Clown of the Parrot World, keas love to play tug-o-war with trekking poles, roll over like dogs, claw each other and destroy any toys they can find.

They are often found on the ski fields too. They stop at nothing.

Once, on a rock overlooking the Rob Roy Glacier high above the Matukituki Valley, some swiss tourists were eating their lunch and admiring the keas on the rocks around them. Suddenly a kea scooped down, hooked his beak into one of the mens' hats, carried it along a bit and dropped it into the deep ravine at the foot of the glacier. Then he disappeared into the swirling alpine mists calling the kea's mischievous laugh: keee-aa, keee-aa, keee-aa.

So although keas were a lot of trouble to the Aspinalls in their early farming days, they also enjoyed the parrots which loved to

mimic the roosters crowing. One was always waiting for them when they came back from town.

John and Amy had two children. There were no local schools Jerry and Pat could go to, but fortunately in 1922 the Government Correspondence School started. They set up a school room with desks and twice a month went to far away Wanaka to pick up the packages with lessons. Years later, when John's son took over the farm, there were regular school broadcasts and occasional camps for his children as well. But like their parents, when it came to High School they went to Dunedin, for although they could have continued with the Correspondence School, their parents felt it was important to be part of a larger group.

Life on a high country station is busy. Spring is the time for lambing and calving. The sheep have to be mustered from the hill country and brought down into the valley to be shorn in the shearing shed. The wool is sorted, packed into bales, and sent to Dunedin.

To encourage the grass and clover to grow better, small planes spread the high mountain areas with fertilizer.

A vegetable garden provides food for the family and their many visitors. Enough has to be frozen for the winter time when nothing grows in the valley.

Aspiring Station also has cattle which, in summer, have to be moved to summer grazing country, higher up in the mountains and brought back to lower levels in autumn or they would die in the harsh winters.

Autumn is the time to make hay for winter feeding, lambs are selected to send to the sale yards and those to be kept are ear tagged and inoculated against various diseases. Then they are moved to their winter place in the lowland pastures near the homestead.

Fruit has to be picked and made into jam, bottled or put into the deep-freeze.

The life of a high country farmer can be very lonely. The sound of wild storms roaring round the mountains, deep snow in winter or swollen rivers can be frightening.

But it is good for everyone to be alone sometimes. Jesus loved quiet and lonely places. The Bible tells us 'Very early in the morning, while it was still dark, Jesus got up, left the house and went off to a solitary place, where he prayed' (Mark 1:35). That was just before He had to make some important decisions about his disciples. We can't easily hear God speaking to us in the busyness of our daily life. We can hear Him much better when we find a quiet place and listen for His voice. Elijah did this too:

once he was very depressed and felt God was far away. In a lonely place, on the top of a mountain, God came to him personally (read 1 Kings 19:11-18), helped him to understand and gave him a new challenge. If you want to know what God's plan is for you, you need to find a quiet lonely place and just listen. Some people find walking in a lonely and peaceful place to be a great time to praise God and thank Him for all His blessings. It often helps to read your Bible for a while or pray when you are walking along. Some years ago a schoolboy went to a Christian camp in a valley like that of the Matukituki River. Lying on the soft grasses after dark he was astonished at the beauty of the stars. He was overcome by the greatness of God who had made them:

'When I consider your heavens, the work of your fingers, the moon and the stars, which you have set in place, what is man that you are mindful of him, the son of man that you care for him? You made him a little lower than the heavenly beings and crowned him with glory and honor. You made him ruler over the works of your hands; you put everything under his feet: all flocks and herds, and the beasts of the field, the birds of the air and the fish of the sea, all that swim the paths of the seas. O LORD, our Lord, how majestic is your name in all the earth!' (Psalm 8:3-9 NIV).

The next morning the boy gave His life to Christ.

There are times when farmers and their families have to go to town. In former days this could be dangerous. The Macphersons had a farm not far away from Mount Aspiring Station. When, in 1893, New Zealand was the first country in the world to give women the vote they took this very seriously. Mrs Macpherson was no exception and determined to go to town to cast her vote in the 1919 general election. She travelled in a small trap pulled by a favourite horse for the journey to Wanaka. Sadly, on her way home, her horse tripped on a submerged stone in the middle of the river, she was thrown into the swift flowing water and drowned.

A very exciting time of the year is the annual Upper Clutha Agriculture and Pastoral Show in Wanaka. This is when farmers visit agricultural displays of fencing materials, building materials, trucks, Land Rovers, tractors, ploughs, cultivators, hay balers, and many other farm implements. Along one side are the pens where the horses and ponies are waiting their turn in the ring to be shown to the crowd. There are sheep pens for different types and breeds of sheep and strongly fenced pens for the cattle. The best animals receive awards.

The highlight for families is the jack russel race. As many as one hundred of these small terriers, each on a lead held by their young owners, line up at the start line. A horse towing an artificial rabbit rides into the ring, the starter's whistle sounds and the dogs are released. The first to catch the rabbit is the winner!

Paul talks about this – in 1 Corinthians 9:24 we read 'You know that many runners enter a race, and only one of them wins the prize.' Athletes work very hard to win races, especially an Olympic crown, but they can be champions only for a short time. Paul reminds us that the crown that God gives is ours forever and everyone of his children can earn one. To win we don't need to chase a rabbit but it is essential that we walk in His ways and obey His commands.

Gold Fever

For about two thirds of the way, the 300 kilometre journey from Wanaka to Dunedin runs along the great Clutha River, past spectacular lakes, wild river gorges, remote desert areas and towering rocky mountains. Nearer Dunedin the landscape changes to rolling green hills and lonely beaches.

When the early settlers first came to Dunedin from Scotland they had no idea that fifteen years later their peaceful city would be overrun by Gold Fever.

It all started in May 1861 when a man named Gabriel Read hit a major gold strike in Gabriel's Gully, near a small town called Lawrence, about an hour out of Dunedin. Gabriel had suspected there would be gold there, but even he was surprised when he looked into a small hole he had dug. There was a nugget of gold, 'shimmering', he said, 'like stars on the Orion on a dark frosty night'. Within an hour he had ten ounces in his pouch. He rushed off to Dunedin and it wasn't long before everyone knew of the strike. Gold Fever was about to hit them.

The first presbyterian settlers had arrived a few years earlier and the church elders weren't very excited about how gold was bewitching their community. But people began to head for Central Otago in droves. One Sunday, it was reported in the newspaper that only the minister and the session clerk were in church; everyone else had gone to look for gold!

By July there were about 150 men at work in Gabriel's Gully and by September about 6,000 people were on the diggings. At first the diggers were mainly Scotsmen, but when the news got round that two travel stained men had brought a heavy, roughly made bag to the gold receiver's office with eighty-seven pounds of gold, hundreds of miners poured in from Australia and China. That gold had come from the other end of the Clutha River, about one hour from Wanaka.

The miners needed wood for buildings and the frameworks for their gold mining cradles. This mainly came from the forests higher up the valleys, such as the Matukituki Valley. Saw mills built in these valleys used steam engines imported from England to drive their mills. The mills processed large logs, dragged down from the mountains, into usable timber. The timber was stacked on the side of the river to 'season' and when the river was right (not to high or too low) the timber would be tied into rafts with flax and floated down the river to the lakes.

About the same time as gold was discovered, coal was found in the Manuherikia Valley and at one time there were as many as thirty coal mines there. Coal was needed for heating and for feeding the steam dredges which carved the gold from the Clutha River.

Getting the gold out was not easy. It had to be sluiced from the beds of rivers and the terraces around them, dug deep in the soil of the valleys, and carved from the granite tops of mountains as high as 2,000 to 3,000 feet above sea level. The climate they had to work in was harsh. In summer it was fiercely hot, with the rock ranges basting in the heat, yet overnight it might snow. In winter it was dangerously cold. Snow melts and rainstorms caused havoc with rapid floods. When flash floods burst down on the gold fields, turbulent torrents often swept the miners away. Some of the goldfields were so remote the miners had to walk long distances to reach them.

Many men who came to look for the precious metal had left their families behind. They lived in very primitive conditions, in rough shacks, in caves under the rocks or in small cottages made from local stone. Often no one would know where they had come from. In 1865 a man called William Rigney discovered the body of a young man on the riverbank. He tried very hard to find out who it was and what he had died from, but never did manage to get any information. Finally, he arranged a funeral for the unknown miner. On a headstone, which he paid for, he put the words: 'Somebody's darling lies buried here'. When he himself died in 1912, he was buried beside 'Somebody's Darling'.

All over, hotels, shops and new towns sprang up as gold fever took hold. The Central Otago town of Alexandra grew into a major centre for miners and the services they needed: transportation by horse and coach, staging houses, shanty type shops, and services such as shoeing for horses. Mail had to be delivered and newspapers came into existence. Banks made special arrangements. Almost overnight Dunedin became the foremost city in New Zealand.

One of the new towns was a little desert town, thirty minutes from Alexandra, with the Biblical name of Ophir (Job 28:16). No one now knows for sure exactly where it was, perhaps in

India, in Arabia or even in Africa. But what we do know is that it was famous for its gold, the finest that could be found. It was a gift for Kings. One wise man brought a gift of gold to Jesus. But the people who rushed to Central Otago with the idea that they would become rich fast were obsessed with the thought of great wealth for themselves. They soon discovered that there was a great price to pay. The life was hard and many died. And very few actually became rich. For them, as Paul wrote to Timothy in 1 Tim 6:10, 'the love of money causes all kinds of trouble. Some people want money so much that they have given up their faith and caused themselves a lot of pain'.

There may not be any gold where you live, but Paul was talking to all of us. Instead of 'gold' use the words 'money' and 'possessions'. Many young people chase after those and, like many coal miners, pay a huge price.

Paul said, 'Timothy, you belong to God, so keep away from all these evil things. Try your best to please God and be like Him. Be faithful, loving, dependable, and gentle" (1 Timothy 6:11). That's his message to us today too.

Courage and Love

The most dangerous place to mine gold was at Campbell's Diggings on the top of the Old Man Range which towers over the Clutha River. The big snow in August 1863 is remembered by a monument in Gorge Creek at the foot of the range.

The only way to get to Campbell's was to climb over the Old Man Range (2,000 metres high) and then across twenty miles of rough trackless wilderness. In the winter of 1863 there was an unusually fierce storm. Blinding blizzards swept the mountain, froze up tracks and obliterated trails. At the time there were around 500 miners working there. It caught them off guard, without food and the proper equipment needed for survival.

When the situation became impossible, with snow piled deep and provisions running out, many set out to cross the rugged range back to Gorge Creek and the packers' town of Chamonix.

There is no sign of the town now, but at that time there were stores, boarding shanties and a blacksmith's shop in the town.

It was from Chamonix that rescue parties went out to try and rescue the men on the range above them. Covered in icicles, they returned with tales of the many miners who had died of exposure in the snow drifts. No one knows exactly how many of the miners died during that storm but it was at least thirty-four and some believe it may have been a hundred.

After this disaster, the government agreed to put snow poles up, so that miners having to come out during snowstorms would be able to find their way. Unfortunately many of the snow poles were stolen by miners and used for firewood or ridge poles or rafters for their huts. Nowadays all that is left of Chamonix is a memorial and some forgotten grave sites.

During that same snowstorm a story of incredible courage in the face of danger earned a fifteen year old boy a place in history. While his name has been lost, his story has not.

He was a young immigrant from Australia who had the job of carrying the mail between the gold fields up and down the Clutha River on horseback. On the 17th of August 1863, he and his horse, with the two mail bags on either side of his saddle, set out as usual from Gabriel's Gully in spite of the fact that it was snowing heavily. The going was rough, but he reached Lawrence on schedule. Ten miles on he stopped at the Flagstaff accommodation house, where he found many stranded packers sitting out the storm which was 'raging with great fury'. The boy was anxious to get the mail through, but while he was courageous, he was not stupid. He knew that to travel alone was asking for trouble. So he was very glad to find Mr Gardiner, a farmer, who needed to return to his station, more than half a day further inland. The two decided to join forces.

The pair set out around noon. The going was unbelievably rough. The snow storm raged around them and they had great difficulty finding their way. The road was obliterated and the miners had stolen the snow poles. They didn't dare stop to rest, because to sit down even for a moment was to die.

They battled on, all through the night. Early the next morning the exhausted pair finally found the farm. Capable hands rubbed them down until feeling returned to their limbs. After some warm food, they lay down and slept for hours.

The next day, another man who had been riding the storm out at the Gardiners' Station, took the mail on to Dunstan, where it arrived only two days later than expected. The settlement rang with the story of the courage of a fifteen year old boy, whose devotion to duty led him to go where men twice his age did not dare.

Among the people looking for gold were many gold miners from the Guangzhou Delta, a poor part of China where the people had become poor because of overpopulation and the Opium Wars. Unlike the Europeans, they worked in groups and they were happy to go to places the Europeans had already worked over. They didn't like to live in tents, but made huts, using any material they could find. One hut near Cromwell had a chimney made out of old billy cans!

Although most of the Europeans resented the Chinese because they worked so hard, there was one man who reached out to them.

Alexander Don was born in a tent on the gold fields of Australia. He was the eldest of the ten children of a gold miner. Because he was bright, his teachers encouraged him to study at night school when he had to leave school early to work on his grandfather's farm. He did so well that when he was fifteen he became a pupil teacher. Then, one day he heard a well known missionary from the Pacific Islands preach and knew that God wanted him to become a missionary himself. There didn't seem to be any Australian Missionary Societies which could use him but he did hear that the Presbyterian Church of Otago and Southland in New Zealand was looking for someone. Alexander found a ship to take him to Dunedin. Soon after meeting with the church leaders, he was asked to be a missionary to the Chinese gold miners on the Otago gold fields. Alexander was quite sure that that was what God wanted him to do.

But first he needed to learn the language most of the miners spoke. For this, the Church sent him to an American mission station in Canton, China. Two years later he came back and trained to be a minister. In 1882 he was finally ready to go and work among the Chinese. He opened the first Chinese mission church in 1883.

Three years later he started his annual summer preaching tours, visiting all the places where Chinese miners worked. He kept careful records of who was where so that he could refresh his memory before each visit. They were often surprised that he remembered all their names. The Chinese welcomed him as a friend and often trusted him with messages for their families and friends. He used to give out tracts and used colourful posters illustrating Scripture with Cantonese text in large characters. He loved the people and led many of them to faith in God.

On one of his trips he met James Shum. James Shum was

born near Guangzhou and came to New Zealand in 1871. Together with some others from his village he opened a claim at Shepherd's Creek near Bannockburn. He didn't make much money but by 1875 he had managed to save the fare home. James got married but had a row with his family and decided to go back to New Zealand. In 1891 he met the Reverend Alexander Don and through his ministry, became a Christian. In 1906 James went back to China where he worked tirelessly for the Lord until his death in 1914.

God had called Alexander Don when he was still young, but thinking about a good career in teaching. Instead he left everything behind and set out into the unknown, believing God had a special work for him to do. No one knows how many

people came to know the Lord through the ministry of this young and courageous man.

Jesus called twelve disciples. They were all busy people, with careers and families. Then Jesus asked them to follow Him. Have you ever thought what this must have meant to them and their families? It would be a difficult and challenging journey with no salaries. For some it would lead to suffering and a painful death. But they knew it was right and they didn't hesitate. We may think we have our future planned, and it may be right, but we must always be ready to follow where He leads us. Sometimes Jesus asks us to do things that make no sense to us. Remember the disciples who were out all night and caught nothing? Jesus told them to cast their nets on the other side.

Today many fishing boats are equipped with scanners to show them what is under the water. That way they know where the fish are. The disciples didn't have that kind of equipment, but after fishing all night and getting no bites they were pretty sure there weren't any fish around. But that wasn't so.

"When he had finished speaking, he said to Simon, 'Put out into deep water and let down the nets for a catch.' Simon answered, 'Master, we've worked hard all night and haven't caught anything. But because you say so, I will let down the nets.' When they had done so, they caught such a large number of fish that their nets began to break" (Luke 5: 4-6 NIV).

Alexander Don 'fished' where God sent him. He could not have imagined that as a result many would come to know Jesus and that he would be remembered for this. Will you fish where God wants you to throw out your net?

New Zealand Map

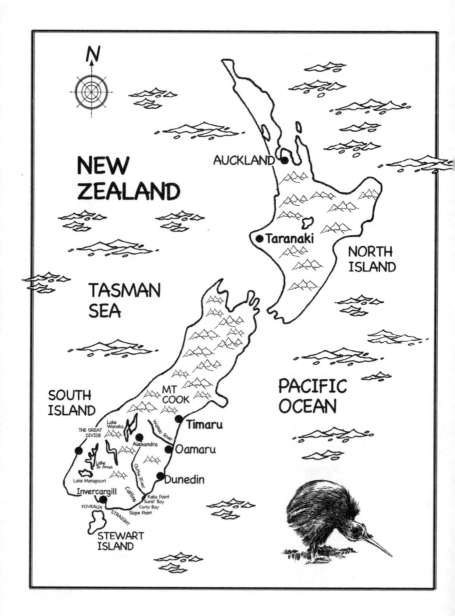

Kiwi Adventures Quiz

1. What two seas does New Zealand lie between?

2. Who did God put in charge of creation in the Garden of Eden?

3. Who do the Kiwis say flew a plane on 1st April 1903?

4. Who didn't believe Joshua and Caleb?

5. From what Scottish town does Dunedin gets its name?

6. What beautiful woman did God use to save the Jews?

7. What speed does an Albatross reach?

8. Who should you rest in and trust?

9. What does the Maori name Hoiho mean?

10. What does Jesus say we should be like - instead of being worriers?

11. What do sea lions love to eat?

12. Who did God tell to be strong and brave?

13. What is a New Zealand Christmas tree?

14. Who did Paul know could be trusted?

15. How big is the brain of a mutton bird?

16. Where did King David ask God to look in order to find out his thoughts?

17. What is the name of the funny parrot that can't fly?

18. Who do all animals and birds belong to?

19. What is the name given to the fungus gnat's larvae?

20. What Israelite leader did not make it to the Promised Land?

21. What bird jumps on a sheep's back to scare it?

22. How do we win God's crown?

23. Who was 'Somebody's Darling'?

24. What place mentioned in the Bible was famous for gold?

25. What caught the miners by surprise in 1863?

26. What language did Alexander Don have to learn in order to tell many miners about Jesus?

Kiwi Adventures Answers

1. The Tasman Sea and The Pacific Ocean.

2. Adam and Eve

3. Richard Pearse

4. The Israelites.

5. Edinburgh.

6. Esther.

7. 115 Kilometres per hour.

8. The Lord God.

9. The bird that shouts.

10. Birds of the sky; wild flowers.

11. Squid.

12. Joshua

13. Pohutukawa.

14. Tychicus.

15. The size of the top of your thumb.

16. In his heart.

17. Kakapo.

18. God.

19. Glow worm.

20. Moses.

21. Kea.

22. Walk in his ways and obey his commands

23. A unknown gold miner who died.

24. Ophir.

25. An unusually fierce storm/blizzard.

26. Chinese.

Adventures with a Mission Flavour

African Adventures by Dick Anderson

Incredible stories from the missionary frontier in Africa.

ISBN 978-1-85792-807-5

Amazon Adventures by Horace Banner

Discover what's it like to live the life of a pioneer missionary.

ISBN 978-1-85792-440-4

Great Barrier Reef Adventures by Jim Cromarty

Explore the Great Barrier Reef and see God's amazing work.

ISBN 978-1-84550068-9

Himalayan Adventures by Penny Reeve

Explore the Himalayas and see God at work in creation.

ISBN 978-1-84550-080-1

Outback Adventures by Jim Cromarty

Encounter Australia's outback and learn about God.

ISBN 978-185792-974-4

Rainforest Adventures by Horace Banner

The Amazon rainforest and its animals point to God's creation.

ISBN 978-185792-627-9

Rocky Mountain Adventures by Betty Swinford

The Rugged Rocky Mountains are breathtaking!

ISBN 978-1-85792962-1

Wild West Adventures by Donna Vann

Wild West stories of animals, scenery and people of faith.

ISBN 978-1-845500-658

Christian Focus Publications publishes books for adults and children under its three main imprints: Christian Focus, Mentor and Christian Heritage. Our books reflect that God's word is reliable and Jesus is the way to know him, and live for ever with him. Our children's publication list includes a Sunday school curriculum that covers pre-school to early teens; puzzle and activity books. We also publish personal and family devotional titles, biographies and inspirational stories that children will love. If you are looking for quality Bible teaching for children then we have an excellent range of Bible story and age specific theological books. From pre-school to teenage fiction, we have it covered!

Find us at our webpage:
www.christianfocus.com